THE FIRST THANKSGIVING

Everybody didn't celebrate Thanksgiving but Grandpa and Grandma always did. It meant a great deal to them because they had been at the First Thanksgiving feast at Plymouth long ago.

In this warm and friendly story of a truly American feast day in a truly American home, Lena Barksdale has succeeded in bringing alive the kindliness and sterling worth of the early settlers.

The delightful illustrations by the well-known artist, Lois Lenski, are as authentic as they are charming.

THE FIRST

Thanksgiving

BY

LENA BARKSDALE

ILLUSTRATED BY LOIS LENSKI

NEW YORK: ALFRED · A · KNOPF

THIS IS A BORZOI BOOK,
PUBLISHED BY ALFRED A. KNOPF, INC.

This title was originally catalogued by the Library of Congress as follows:

Barksdale, Lena. The first Thanksgiving, by Lena Barksdale, illustrated by Lois Lenski.

1. Thanksgiving day. 1. Lenski, Lois, illus. II. Title

L.C. Catalog Card Number: 42-21306

ISBN: 0-394-91156-3 (Lib. ed.)

To

DAVID AND CAROLINE HOGARTH

who, like the Pilgrims, are both

English and American

Sarah
Conklin

THE FIRST THANKSGIVING

CHAPTER ONE

Hannah snuggled down in the big feather bed, and pulled the quilts close under her chin. She was tired and a little sleepy, although she was so excited about what had happened today, and what was going to happen tomorrow, and the bed felt so good and soft and fresh—not like the hard bunk on Brother Paul's boat that had brought her to Gloucester from Maine, and not a bit like that musty old bed she had slept in at the ordinary last night. She would have slept in this nice bed last night too, but the cart broke down just a few miles away, so she and Uncle Jonathan had slept at the ordinary, and waited for the blacksmith to mend the wheel. It didn't take long, once the blacksmith got his fires going

[3

this morning, and just an hour after sunrise they were on their way.

Hannah opened her eyes and looked across at the tiny loft window, where the moonlight made the heavy greased paper that took the place of glass look like a blurry patch on the dark wall. Glass was expensive and hard to get, and Hannah thought it was wonderful that they had glass in the windows downstairs. There was no glass in the windows of the small frontier house in Maine where she had spent most of her nine years. At home, John and Henry slept in the loft, and she slept downstairs in the trundle bed that was kept under Mother's big bed in the daytime. She had always thought it would be fun to climb the ladder and sleep in the loft, and that is just what she would do here at Uncle Jonathan's, where there were two loft rooms. Timothy had one and the girls the other. And here was Content on one side of her in the big bed and Mercy on the other, her cousins whom she never saw before today. Just think, two girls to play with! There were only the two boys at home, and they were so much older than she was. They carved toys for her sometimes by the fire in the long winter evenings, but they had to keep Mother's wood box filled and help Father too, and they didn't have much time to play. Now she had here two cousins. Content was eight and Mercy ten, and she was between them in age, just as she was lying between them in the big bed.

They had been so surprised to see her when Uncle Jonathan drove up to the door and called them to come and get the fine present he'd brought them—meaning her. She got out of the cart, a little cramped and cold and more than a little shy, because she didn't know whether Aunt Hattie and the children would want to see her as much as she wanted to see them. But they did, and they liked her! She smiled in the darkness, wide awake now, but careful not to bounce a little with happiness, as she wanted to do, because she knew Mercy and Content were both asleep. Instead she put out a hand on each side and touched them softly while she remembered how Aunt Hattie had untied her hood, smoothed her hair and said they were so glad to have her come to stay with them this winter. Slipping out of her warm homespun cloak, Hannah had looked around the bright cosy kitchen. Then Content took her hand and led her to a stool close to the fire while Mercy ran to get rye cakes still warm from the oven. Aunt Hattie gave each one a mug of milk, and they toasted their feet by the fire as they ate their lunch.

They all laughed merrily about how Hannah had ridden from Gloucester on top of the sugar and molasses in Uncle Jonathan's ox cart, but it wasn't funny, really. Hannah explained that the bolt of calico that Uncle Jonathan had set across two barrels made a very good seat, except when

the cart jolted too much. Anyway, she spent most of the time tripping along by Uncle Jonathan's side, or running ahead of the oxen. She was much warmer that way, and besides she could open and close the gates that they had to pass through, unless the catch was too high or the gate too heavy. Uncle Jonathan had talked to her just as though she were a grown-up person. He said that someday he hoped there would be roads wide enough and smooth enough for chaises and coaches drawn by good horses all through the colony, instead of traces in the woods and cart roads through the farms. But he said people were so busy picking rocks out of their own fields that they didn't take time to go out and clear a real road, and that meant that travelers must open and shut gates and go the long way around to reach their destination. Hannah knew that before she became a traveler herself she wouldn't have been interested in that kind of thing, but yesterday she and Uncle Jonathan had chatted about roads at a great rate, and she had found it all right interesting. Then when one of the big wheels of the ox cart got caught

The First Thanksgiving

in a deep rut, "once too often," Uncle Jonathan said, and the oxen in pulling the wheel loose ground it against a boulder and broke it, Uncle Jonathan merely said, "Now, child, you see how ruinous it is to a poor farmer not to have a proper road to market." That was why they had to wait another whole day to get home.

When Hannah arrived, Aunt Hattie was busy making a pudding to take to Grandma, and the spices smelt so good and homey in the warm kitchen. Aunt Hattie and the girls said they were so glad she had come in time to go with them to Grandpa's tomorrow for the family Thanksgiving. Hannah shivered a little when she remembered how close she had come to missing that big yearly event. Mother told her about it every year, but they lived much too far away to go. Why, Mother hadn't even seen Grandma and Grandpa since she married Father and went to Maine to live. That was ever so long ago. Mother must have had it in mind for a long time to send her to Uncle Jonathan's, Hannah realized, although it was unusual to send a little girl so far from home when travel was difficult

and often dangerous. If Mother ever longed to
visit her relatives no one ever knew it, but she
seemed to be determined to have Hannah spend
a year with them, and the only question was how
to get her there. Then suddenly Brother Paul
who was old Captain Bartlett's mate, was made
captain of the brig *Nancy*, with orders to take
a cargo of lumber out of Kittery, Maine, to
Gloucester. Fortunately he had a free day before sailing, and he was so excited about being
made captain that he borrowed a horse and rode
out to the farm to tell the family about it. Mother

said at once that Hannah should go with him. "And how will she get from Gloucester to Jonathan's?" asked Father. "Paul won't have time to hire a horse and go gallivanting over the country to take her there." "There'll be a way," Mother had answered, "else she can come back with Paul, and no harm done."

And, sure enough, there was a way. Brother Paul had met Uncle Jonathan near the wharf the very morning after the *Nancy* reached port. Uncle Jonathan had come to town with his ox cart full of farm truck to trade for store goods. He came straight on board the *Nancy* to see her, and smiled and said in his slow funny way that he hadn't counted on taking a fine lady traveling in his ox cart, but that if she didn't mind going that way he'd be downright pleased to have her. So early the next morning Hannah, perched on top of the calico and the other boughten goods, rode behind the oxen as they slowly plodded out of Gloucester. Uncle Jonathan had told her right away that she would be in time to go to the harvest feast at Grandpa's. Of course, Mother had hoped she would arrive in time, but none of them knew just when Thanksgiving would be. It all depended on the crops and the weather and Grandma's rheumatism, and they couldn't possibly know about those things way off in Maine. Somehow Hannah just knew she would arrive in time, and sure enough she had. Tomorrow was the day, and Aunt Hattie had sent the children to bed right after an early supper so they would be ready for a very early start in the morning. Hannah remembered a little guiltily that they were supposed to go right to sleep, as Content and Mercy had done, while she had been so busy thinking about all the wonderful

things that had happened and were going to happen that she had completely forgotten what Aunt Hattie had said. Hannah always liked to think things over after she went to bed, except when she had been cross, or had done things that she shouldn't have done. Tonight there were only nice things to think about.

Thanksgiving Day! Mother said she mustn't ever forget that it meant more than having a big dinner, more even than eating it at Grandpa's, which she would do tomorrow for the first time. It meant being thankful for all the nice, happy things in your life, and she certainly had a great many things to be thankful for tonight. Why, just think, it wouldn't be tiresome to sit quietly working at her knitting and her sampler this winter with Mercy and Content working at theirs, and all three chatting by the fire! If only Mother and Father and the boys could be here too. Mother knew that Hannah never had any other little girls to play with, and that she was often lonely, and that was why she wanted her to come to Uncle Jonathan's. But more than anything else she had wanted Hannah to spend

Thanksgiving with Grandpa and Grandma. Everybody didn't celebrate Thanksgiving, Hannah knew, but Grandpa and Grandma always did. It meant a great deal to them because they had been at that First Thanksgiving feast at Plymouth many years ago, when Massasoit and his braves came to make merry with their new white neighbors. Grandma would tell them all about that tomorrow, if she felt well enough. She always told about it, Mother said, because she wanted her children and grandchildren to remember that First Thanksgiving always, and to go on celebrating it every year. Goodness, the moonlight has gone off that window! It must be 'way in the night, and Aunt Hattie said to go right to sleep. Well, she would now. She wouldn't think about another thing!

CHAPTER TWO

The next morning, at early dawn, Aunt Hattie called the children to come and eat their porridge. Timothy, who had just finished milking, came in to join them. Hannah stirred her porridge absent-mindedly.

"Content," she said suddenly, "what does Grandma look like?"

Content looked at Hannah in astonishment. "Why," she said, "Grandma just looks like Grandma."

Timothy grinned at his little sister. "But Content," he said, "Hannah doesn't know what Grandma looks like. She's never seen her, you know, and she wants you to tell her."

"Oh," said Content, smiling, " 'course; I forgot. Grandma's little, Hannah, 'bout as big as Mercy, maybe. She's got bright eyes and lots of wrinkles, and she walks bent over her stick, 'cause she's got rheumatism, you know."

Hannah nodded. "And what's Grandpa like?"

"Grandpa's sort of big. No, not very big," said Content, warming up to her description, " 'cause he's powerful old, you know. He and Grandma are the oldest folks hereabouts, but Father says he's spry for his age. Grandpa won't talk very much, but he keeps apples and hickory nuts and butternuts in his pockets that he gives

us children. We love to go to see Grandpa and Grandma, and sometimes Grandma tells us 'bout the Pilgrims and the First Thanksgiving."

"Well, daughter," said Uncle Jonathan, who had come into the room while Content was talking, "I think Hannah knows pretty well what to expect now. I hope Grandpa has laid in a good supply of apples for all of you. Timothy, see if your mother is ready, while I rake the fire. Get your cloaks, children. We should be on our way."

In a few minutes they had started. Content rode in front of her father on his big gray horse, and Hannah was perched on the pillion behind Aunt Hattie, who had the pudding for Grandma, well wrapped and tied to the pummel of her saddle. Timothy and Mercy rode together on another horse. They were all in holiday mood, laughing and singing as they trotted briskly along the well-worn trace through the woods. Hannah was enjoying her ride immensely. It was ever so much faster than ox cart travel, and a great deal nicer.

"There's the house, dear, just beyond those

trees," said Aunt Hattie. "You can see it better in a minute."

Hannah craned her neck for a better view around Aunt Hattie's elbow, and fairly gasped in astonishment at what she saw. She was sure she had never seen a house half as big before! It stood on a gentle slope, and was almost square, with heavy clapboards weathered to a soft gray. Its overhang supported a full second story, with attic above. Smoke curled from the large central chimney, and the sunshine, striking full on its double tier of windows, gave the house a festive air. On the right there was a gigantic elm, through whose bare branches Hannah could see a corner of the barn. On the left there were many other trees, bordering a brook now frozen over.

The horses clattered over the bridge above the brook, and in another minute the riders were dismounting before the massive front door. The big room they entered was known as the Hall, Hannah discovered later, and it seemed to be full of people already. Hannah had to greet so many aunts and uncles and cousins whom she had never

seen before that she felt completely bewildered
by the time Aunt Hattie took her hand and led
her over to a little old lady in a white cap and
snowy kerchief, sitting close by the fireplace.

"Here's Hannah, Mother, Abby's child, you
know, from Maine. She came yesterday. Hannah, this is your grandmother."

"God bless you, dear child," said Grandma in
her sweet, soft voice. "You've come a long journey, but we are people who make long journeys.
Your grandpa was but a lad and I a young lass
when we crossed the Atlantic long ago. Nowa-
days your Uncle William travels to far places in
his ship. Your mother went far away with your

father, and you return to visit us. That is well, and I am sure we are all right pleased to have you here among so many of your kin. Come closer, and let Grandma look at you. A big girl you are, like your dear mother when she was your age."

"Let's have a look at Abby's lass!" said a deep voice, and there was Grandpa, tilting Hannah's head back, so that he could look into her deep blue eyes. "Do they feed you well 'way off there in the Province of Maine, little one? Here's a red apple from Grandpa, the reddest one from my best tree! Eat it. Long time before dinner."

"Thank you, Grandpa," murmured Hannah, but Grandpa was gone already, his ample pockets bulging with apples for the other children.

"Is your mother well, my child, and your father and your brothers? Is all well at your home? We remember all of you daily in our family prayers."

"Yes, Grandma, Mother is well, and the boys are 'most as big and strong as Father."

"It would comfort my old eyes to see them, but their work is elsewhere, and you are their messenger on this good day. You are very welcome, Hannah. Come, Mercy! Content! You children take Hannah around and show her everything. Run out to the barn and see the new kittens before you take your things off. Hannah, you may have one of the kittens to take home with you."

"Oh, Grandma! I'd like a kitten for my own. Thank you."

"Well, run along, child, and choose the one you like best."

Munching apples happily, the three little girls started to go through the kitchen on their way to the barn. As Mercy opened the kitchen door Hannah's eyes almost popped out of her head at the sight of five tall, solemn Indians, resplendent in feathers and flowing robes. They were standing like statues around the huge fireplace where preparations for dinner were going forward as rapidly as circumstances would permit. Dilly, the cook, and her helpers had no choice but to dodge Indians on their errands about the kitchen. The Indians, having posted themselves where they wished to stand, never moved an inch, and seemed to be unaware of the bustling activity.

Hannah turned wildly, and catching sight of Aunt Hattie, she ran to her, caught her hand and almost sobbed, "Oh, Aunt Hattie! Come quick! The kitchen's full of big Indians."

"That's all right, Hannah, dear, don't you worry," said Aunt Hattie soothingly. "They won't hurt us. Don't you know Grandpa and Grandma feed as many Indians as want to come on Thanksgiving? Indians came to the First Thanksgiving, you know, and Grandpa and Grandma want them to keep on coming. If everyone was as good and kind as Grandpa and Grandma, we'd never have any trouble with In-

dians, I am sure. You go on now with Mercy and Content. There'll be plenty more Indians outside probably, but they won't hurt you. I am sure I don't know how Dilly and the girls ever get the dinner cooked, bobbing around Indians to baste the roast, but nothing would make those Indians stir out of anybody's way until they see their food coming."

Somewhat reassured, Hannah allowed Mercy and Content to lead her through the kitchen, past the Indians who stood in dignified silence with folded arms, and paid no more attention to the children than they did to the scurrying cooks. Once outside on the neat path leading to the barn, Mercy giggled and said, "If I was Dilly, I'd spill something hot on those old Indians and make them move out of the way."

Content didn't think that would do at all, and they were still arguing about it when they reached the barn, where Uncle Jonathan and Timothy were putting up the horses.

The girls soon found the kittens, and Hannah almost forgot about the Indians in her delight at the thought of having a pet of her own. It was so hard to decide between a gray kitten with a white apron under its chin and a lively little black one with four white feet! Then Uncle Jonathan was smiling down at them, and Timothy called, "Come on, girls, leave those old cats, and let's go see how many Indians are waiting in the pasture this time!"

"They are not old cats! They are darling kittens," cried Content, indignantly, "and Hannah's going to have one of her own. Grandma said so!"

"All right!" said Timothy, good-naturedly, "but they'll keep. Don't you want to see if Banto is here with his animals?"

"Oh, yes!" said Mercy. "Come on, Content and Hannah! You know," she added, turning to Hannah, "Banto is an Indian boy who knows how to tame animals, little ones, of course, whose mothers have been killed. He's had bear cubs, and all kinds of wild things, and they follow him around."

"Yes, until they get tired of staying around the camp and run off to the woods," said Timothy. "They always do, but by that time Banto has found some other cub to take care of. Well, are you coming?"

"Go on, children," said Uncle Jonathan, "play with the Indians for a while. Nothing would please your Grandfather more."

Hannah looked at him appealingly. "Afraid of Indians, child?" he asked, kindly. "These Indians won't hurt you. Not on your Grandpa's place, they won't. Your Grandpa's got a way with Indians. He seems to understand them, and maybe they understand him—I don't know. But the squaws and children out in the pasture are all right. They are going to have a rousing good dinner, and they know it. Go along and see them."

So Hannah went along. It seemed to be the thing that everybody expected her to do, but Indians gave her such a scary feeling. She certainly didn't want to go and see any more of them.

She didn't see how you could help being afraid of Indians. They were so wild and strange, and they did such dreadful things to people sometimes. Hannah's nearest neighbors were some distance away, and she knew very well that when she and her mother were at home alone, as they often were, when Father and the boys were off in the woods cutting timber or hunting, no matter how busy Mother was with her spinning or weaving she never forgot to look around the clearing now and then to see that all was well, although she never said a word about being afraid. Hannah had a favorite place that she liked to play around the roots of a big tree near the creek the other side of the meadow, but she knew without being told that she must never go that far from the house when she and Mother were alone. "The Indians have never molested us," Mother used to say, "and, please God, they never will." But sometimes travelers stopped to spend the night and told terrible stories of Indian raids and of people being carried off captive, and often their families and friends never knew what happened to them. Mother would send Hannah to bed if the stories were very bad, but though you didn't mean to eavesdrop, sometimes you couldn't help hearing the talk if you weren't asleep. Hannah didn't worry too much about those stories, but she had a perfectly natural fear of Indians, and other people that she knew at home felt very much the same way, so she couldn't understand why so many Indians should have the run of Grandpa's place, nor why everyone accepted it so calmly.

However, when they came in sight of the squaws, squatting by the bubbling pots over their campfires, obviously in high good humor, while the children played and ran races around the big pasture, even Hannah could see that there was really nothing to be afraid of. Maybe the Indians here were much tamer than they were where she came from. She didn't want the others to think she was a coward. She'd keep

close beside her cousins, and do whatever they did.

They found Banto with a tame crow on his shoulder and two lively little animals playing at his feet.

"Wolf cub," grunted Banto in reply to a question from Timothy. "Banto tame like dog. Grow big, run fast."

Timothy was playing with the cubs, holding a stout stick for them to snap at. "Yes," he said, "if they don't run away first. How'd you tame that crow?"

"Him hurt wing. Banto fix. Him like Banto."

The crow cocked his beady eyes at the white children and flapped his wings uneasily. Banto produced a handful of acorn meats which the crow picked daintily out of his hand.

The girls watched him for a while, and then their attention was caught by a game that the bigger boys were playing with racquets and balls. Timothy joined some of the older cousins who had come down from the house, and they made up two teams, one of white boys and one of Indians. There was much running to and fro, and the girls were pleased to see that Timothy was as skilful as any of the others in balancing the ball in the racquet and eluding his opponents who were trying to take it away from him.

"I'm cold," said Content, "and tired standing still all this time watching those boys. Let's us play tag with the Indian children."

So away they went, and it wasn't long before they were rosy and breathless. A little later they heard the big bell at the house calling them to dinner and they had to scamper fast to reach the house in time to make themselves neat for the meal.

CHAPTER THREE

The three little girls made a pleasant picture as they stood holding hands at the door of the Hall, their faces shining from a hasty scrubbing and their eyes bright with excitement. They had on their best dresses of linsey woolsey with dainty kerchiefs folded demurely beneath their chins. Hannah's dress was green, Mercy's was russet and Content's plum-colored. Across the Hall in the huge fireplace blazing logs crackled merrily. Through the middle of the room stretched a long table of hewn boards supported by trestles and covered with snowy lengths of homespun linen. Around the head of the table chairs were placed for the older people, and at the foot there were stools and benches for the children. The

[29

most delicious smell of roast turkey, roast duck
and steaming venison pie filled the room.
Enough to make anybody hungry, thought
Hannah, but, gracious! she was hungry already,
and she couldn't begin to see half the good things
that were on that table! Grandpa and Grandma
were already seated at the head in their Governor Carver chairs, so the little girls went forward, suddenly feeling shy, and curtsied nicely
to their grandparents before they found their
own places at the other end of the table. When
the bustle of finding places was over, Grandpa
asked a simple blessing, the uncles carved the

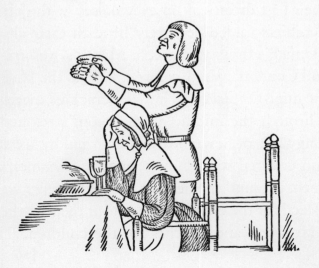

meat, and dinner began in a pleasant buzz of talk. Hannah knew, of course, that the children must be quiet. If they talked at all among themselves they must speak very softly in order not to disturb the conversation of their elders, and, unless they were spoken to, it would never occur to them to ask questions or to join in the conversation. So she settled down blissfully to the quiet enjoyment of her good dinner. She saw that besides the other meat there was a whole pig roasted, with an apple in its mouth. There was a quantity of hominy, parsnips, succotash, beans, stewed cranberries, onions and turnips. The older people had cider or ale, and there were mugs of rich milk for the younger children. There were puddings and several kinds of pies and those who liked imported sweets could have their choice of suckets, comfits, candied ginger and rock candy. Dilly saw to it that the children were well supplied with everything.

When the edge was off Hannah's hunger she remembered the five Indians in the kitchen and wondered if they were still there. Yes, indeed, by stretching up a little she could see them plainly through the kitchen door. They were squatting near the fireplace, still wrapped in their robes, with trenchers piled with food before them, eating away for dear life. Timothy whispered to her that they would think it far beneath their dignity to eat outside with the squaws and children.

Hannah shook her head in bewilderment. She couldn't see why they thought themselves so important, but then she supposed she would never understand Indians. What was it Uncle Jonathan had said in the barn about Grandpa understanding them? She looked the length of the table at Grandpa's fine old face, with many wrinkles around the eyes that twinkled as he listened to something Aunt Hattie was saying to him. Yes, he certainly looked wise and kind, too, and she was so glad that she, his little granddaughter from 'way off in Maine, was here today, sitting at his table for the first time in her life. A ray of sunshine came in through the tiny panes of the window opposite and touched his white hair and Grandma's cap, and Hannah knew that she would remember that picture of them always. She would go back home and tell her mother just how they looked, and maybe years and years later she'd tell her children and even her grandchildren about them too, and about this Thanksgiving feast at their house. Hannah was having such a wonderful time thinking about the present and the far-distant future that she didn't realize dinner was over until Content pulled her sleeve and told her to come on and not to sit there all day!

Right after dinner, Mercy and Content got Grandma's permission to show Hannah over the house. They enjoyed pointing out the panelling in the Hall that "Grandpa carved and put up with his own hands long ago when he first built the house." Grandpa had made some of the chairs too, and he made the big settle when he and Grandma were first married. Hannah was particularly impressed with the real stairway which led up to full-size rooms on the second floor. It all seemed very fine to her, as indeed it was, in contrast with the smaller rooms and loft stories of simpler homes. There was an attic above the second story, and Hannah felt that

she had climbed to a dizzy height when she looked out of the attic window and saw a considerable sweep of fields and woodland stretching away in the distance.

"Look!" she exclaimed, "there's the pasture where we played this morning, and the Indians are still eating their dinner!"

"Yes, and over there," said Mercy, pointing in the other direction, "is the way we came from home. You can see the trace through the woods plainly now that the leaves are off the trees."

"We can't see your house, can we, Mercy?"

"No, it's much too far away, about a mile the other side of that hill. We'd better go down now. Grandma will begin her story soon."

"Thank you for showing me everything, 'specially the attic," said Hannah, "I do like so much being up here above everything."

"If you are here next summer we can come back up here and you'll be 'sprized to see how different everything looks—so much closer and all."

Chatting happily together, the girls went slowly downstairs.

Hannah decided to sit quietly on a stool in the Hall for a while and try to sort out the various relatives whom she had met for the first time that morning. That was Aunt Joy, Uncle William's wife, helping the servants clear away the meal. Hannah liked Aunt Joy. There was something about Aunt Joy—the way she moved maybe or her sweet smile, Hannah couldn't quite decide which—that reminded her of her mother. Aunt Joy and the five boys lived with Grandpa and Grandma, Hannah knew, because Uncle

William was a sea captain and had to be away
most of the time. She was so glad he could be at
home this Thanksgiving. It was not hard to pick
him out; he was big and talkative and merry, and
his twinkling blue eyes in his tanned weather-
beaten face looked as though they could see a
long way over dancing waves or storm-tossed
seas. Then there was Uncle Gilbert, and the lady
in the fine dress must be Aunt Pauline. Uncle
Gilbert had been to Harvard College and he was
a judge and a very important man in the colony,
but Hannah didn't think he looked as kind as
Uncle Jonathan or as much fun as Uncle Wil-

liam. He and Aunt Pauline had ridden horseback from Boston yesterday.

The tall slender young man was Cousin Peter, and Timothy said he was a trader and that sometimes he went out into the Indian country and stayed for weeks, and if there should be trouble with the Indians he would make a fine scout. Timothy hoped that next year he could go out with Cousin Peter and learn the business. There were many things that a boy could do to make himself useful to a trader, he said. Cousin Susan and Cousin Faith were Cousin Peter's sisters. They were Mother's and Uncle Jonathan's

cousins, but much younger. That proper-look-
ing gentleman sitting by Cousin Susan must be
Master Richard Wentworth. Mercy said they
were going to be married in the spring, and
Hannah hoped she could go to the wedding.

There were several other grownups, but
Hannah couldn't remember who they were, and
she hadn't time to find out just now because
Uncle William was telling a story and everyone
was listening. Uncle William was standing by
the fire with his long pipe in one hand and a
tankard of ale in the other, and Hannah thought
he looked every inch a sea captain with his red-
dish hair tossing in confusion over his well-set
head and his eyes flashing with excitement. Hannah noticed that Timothy was drinking in every
word, and she giggled a little to herself and wondered if Timothy would decide now that he
would like to go to sea as cabin boy on Uncle
William's ship instead of going trading with
Cousin Peter. She knew she'd much rather go
to sea than to go off and trade with the Indians,
but of course she was just a girl and couldn't plan
to do anything exciting. Making a sampler and

learning how to spin and weave and make candles and soap seemed very dull now when Uncle William was telling about the far-off places he had visited, and battening down for storms and all the other strange things you had to do on a ship. What's that he's saying now? Something about being chased by a pirate, and he thought he was "a goner sure that time. The brigantine," he continued, "a wicked-looking vessel she was, was coming up fast. We'd crowded on all sail and could do no more. We had a sweet little cargo which we'd no mind to lose, nor our skins neither, for that matter, so we would have put up a good fight if they had overhauled us. We were close enough to see the villains on deck with their cutlasses in their teeth and the grappling irons ready to heave on to our deck. Our lookout had sighted a ship some time before. How the pirates missed it I don't know, but there it was in full view, coming on fast, and that gave the villains something to think about. A big ship it was coming straight at them with its guns ready for action, and a brave sight to me and my men. The pirates were all for getting away then. They

thought we were such easy prey that they hadn't
bothered to reload their cannon, after their shot
at us went wild, and now it must have got stuck.
Many pirates are good seamen and good gunners,
too, but fortunately for us this was but a poor
crew, so we were able to block their flight while
the other ship came up and got within range.
They let the pirates have it and in a short time,
between us, we had a nice prize to sail into Boston Harbour. The other ship was the *Falcon*,
Captain Harvey, out of Liverpool with a cargo
for Boston merchants. A fine fellow. I asked him
to come and visit us, Father, but business keeps
him in Boston."

"Your friends are always welcome, Son. I'm
sorry he couldn't come," said Grandpa.

"Now, William," said Aunt Joy, "no more
sea tales for the present. It is time for Mother to
tell her Thanksgiving story to the children, and
I notice none of us older folk ever want to miss
a word of it, either," she continued with a smile,
as she straightened the rug over Grandma's lap.

CHAPTER FOUR

"I am ready to begin," said Grandma. "Where's Hannah? Come here, child, and sit on this stool at my feet. It's where your mother used to sit, my dear, when she was your age, and you must sit here today, and hear your old Grandmother tell about Thanksgiving in Pilgrim days.

"It was a long time ago, my children, that First Thanksgiving, as we like to call it, though people have always given thanks for good harvests, I am sure, and they always will. But this first feast of ours in Plymouth more than forty years ago was different, I think, from any other harvest feast ever held before, or any that can ever be held again. I want the sweet memory of it to go down in our family long after I am gone,

[41

through you to your children and grandchildren, so I am going to try to tell you something about what our first year in America was like, as well as about the harvest feast that came at the end of that year.

"Your grandfather and I were little more than children then, but we could work along with the older people. Every pair of hands counted, and if some were a little smaller none made note of it. There was much work to be done. We did what we could gladly. We'd had a long voyage, and many good people died of a strange sickness on the ship. We had thought to land in Virginia, where there were many English settlers before us. It might well be that they would be pleased to see us, and would gladly show us how to make our homes snug and comfortable against the cold, and teach us the ways of this new land. But God had other plans for us. In His wisdom He brought us here to a rocky, bleak, frozen land, as it seemed to us then, lying in stretches of desolate shore, empty of houses, where there was no one to welcome us.

"We lived on the ship for many weeks, but as

soon as it seemed reasonably safe we women were set ashore to wash our linen, which sorely needed cleansing after our tedious voyage. It was good to feel solid earth under our feet again, but we dared not venture far, nor go out of sight of our protectors, for none knew where the savages were, or how they might greet us. The men would go forth in parties armed with their muskets, taking the long boat or the shallop, and landing here and there to spy out the land and find a fair place to build our town. We women on the ship could only pray for their safe return when they ventured forth. They

would be gone sometimes one day, often two days or more, and we had no way to gauge the dangers that might surround them. They always returned, though such was the hazard and discomfort of the journey that their clothes were ofttimes frozen to them, in the bitter cold and wet. They found wood and water aplenty and certain places cleared where corn had been planted, and in one place they found great store of corn buried in the ground. Much of that they brought back with them meaning to make full satisfaction to the owners when they could meet and parley with them.

"Once when some of the men were returning to the ship they brought a boatload of juniper boughs that they had cut. We burned it in our stoves, taking comfort in the spicy smell of it. That was our first welcoming from the land.

"At last the men came to an agreement where to build the town, and they set to cutting down trees to build the houses, each man working diligently, and at last the day came when we were all set ashore, with our gear, and the ship sailed away and left us. We were often cold, and

hungry and afraid that winter, but we got along.
. . . Later, you know, Squanto came and lived
with us for a time, and he taught us to plant the
corn when the oak leaf was the size of a mouse's
ear, and as we planted the seed, he had us throw
two fish in each hole to enrich the soil, so that the
yield would be more abundant. He caught good
eels for us, and taught us many other things, useful for us to know. We could not have known
many of these things otherwise, our lives having
been so different in Holland, and before that,
in England. Do not forget, my children, it was
an Indian who first befriended us and guided us

in the new land. Massasoit, their sagamore, also became our friend and made a treaty of peace with us.

"In the sweet spring weather I'll never forget how comforting it was to see the trees come into leaf, and the little wild flowers blooming along the streams and in the woods. We found onions and watercress, fresh and tasty to the palate. One fair day, when my stint of work was done, I was walking beyond the village street, enjoying the sweet fresh air and the smell of blossoms. Your grandfather came down the trail, and led me to a strip of meadow that he had just noticed. It was covered with a thick mat of strawberries. We ate a few and picked many to carry home with us. Strange it is how I remember the taste

of those strawberries all these years. The smell of that juniper on the ship, the tang of water-cress, and the sweetness of wild strawberries— it was such simple things as these that made us begin to love the land, and feel at home at last.

"So it was that by the time our first harvest was ripe and gathered into the storing sheds that we had provided, we knew beyond any doubt that we had found a good comfortable land where we were free and could live our lives without anyone meddling. That's the great thing, children, and don't any of you forget it. God has given us freedom here to think and to worship as seems right to us. Remember to be upright in all your dealings with one another and with the Indians. Be true to God and honest and kind to your neighbor. That is what being free means, and if we forget it we shall suffer, and rightly so. Your grandpa's been true and fine all his long life, and so must you children be."

Grandma's eyes were very bright and her voice shook a little as she looked into the faces of her strong sons and daughters and all the grandchildren, sitting around her crackling fire.

After a moment she went on:

"Then when the first harvest was in and we knew none would go hungry that winter, nor cold, because our houses were built of stout timbers and there was great store of wood to burn, our governor and the other men decided we would have a feast and invite Massasoit to come and bring some of his braves to eat it with us. They set a day, and sent a messenger to invite Massasoit who was pleased to accept, and who sent five deer as a gift toward the feast. For days all the women and girls were busy roasting and baking and shining the pewter. The boys cut many fresh trenchers from stout poplar wood, and spoons too, though we knew our guests would not bother overmuch with spoons, preferring to use their fingers. The men brought in wild turkey, geese and duck in abundance, as well as deer. Your grandfather brought down his first deer and that was a proud day for him. We had found cranberries growing wild that summer, and the women found ways of using them, and our harvest had yielded plenty of corn, some of which we had laboriously ground for bread, and some we had cracked for hominy. We were so happy preparing the food for that feast. You never know how wonderful it is to have plenty all 'round you until you've gone hungry as we went hungry that first winter. So we set about preparing a lavish abundance of food for our guests, but we didn't know how many guests were coming."

Grandma smiled, and the older people chuckled. They knew how many guests had come!

"It's just as well we didn't know," she went on, "we couldn't have worked any harder, and we would have worried for fear we didn't have enough. Such a good smell of roasting and baking filled the village as put us all in fine humor. Maybe Massasoit and his men smelt that good smell away off in their town. Anyway, ninety of them came, and I was the first to see them. It happened this way:

"We brought our food together at the common house that morning, all the victuals that had been cooked in the several houses where the most skilful housewives lived. We women had

put on our best caps and fresh kerchiefs, and we were busily laying out the trenchers when some-one remembered a basket of fresh loaves left by mistake in one of the more distant houses. I was sent to fetch it, and as I came out of the door with the basket on my arm, I looked across the fields and saw our guests coming down the trail from the woods. Of course we were used to the Indians and their outlandish ways of dressing by that time, and I thought not at all about how different they were from us, but only that they made a brave and proper sight. Tall, strong men they were, some with feathers stuck in the bands around their heads. Their long straight hair shone with bear's grease. They wore deerskins over their shoulders, and some wore long tight hose that met the leather girdles around their waists. A few had their faces painted in black or red or yellow, to suit each man's fancy. I could see the wildcat skin that one important brave had thrown over his arm. I could tell Massasoit a great way off because of the heavy chain of white bone beads that he was wont to wear

around his neck. He was also wearing the copper chain with a jewel in it that our people gave him when he first visited us many months before. They came along the trail, single file as was their custom, and as I watched I saw more and more coming, until it seemed to me, in my foolish fancy, that all the Indians in America were coming to our feast. Then as I stood there idly watching, it came over me that no one else in the town had seen them, and I ran to the common house as fast as I could because I knew our elders must be warned in time to go out and greet them properly.

"All the people were dismayed to learn my news, and we were much put to it to welcome our guests and serve them graciously, for we could never let them suspect that we had looked for no more than a score. We bustled around and prepared more tables out of doors. Fortunately, it was not excessively cold. Anyway, we were used to the cold and of course they were. We had built fires outside to take off the chill, and the best carpet and cushions for their principal men were ready to be spread. So by the

time the Indians had got through passing that smelly pipe of theirs around among themselves and our men, the food was ready, and our guests were more than ready to eat it. But of course if you didn't know them, you would never have guessed it. It was their habit to move slowly and deliberately, as if they were pretending the food was not there until the time came to fall to. Never in all my life have I seen so many people eat so much. Those Indians must have been hollow to the knees. One big brave grabbed a whole turkey and gnawed away at it until there was nothing left but bare bones. Then he was ready to begin on a steak of venison, which he ate along with two or three tankards of beer. He finished off with a whole pie. Truly the food melted away that day, but there was plenty left for us women when we got a chance to eat.

"Later on they wrestled, ran races, sang, danced and played games, probably some of the same games that you children played this morning. The Indians could outrun and outwrestle our boys, but when our boys began teaching the Indians some of our English games the Indians didn't win so often. It wouldn't have been wise to let them think they could beat us in everything. It was a great day, and our guests liked it so well that they wrapped up in their deerskins and spent the night in the town, and the next day, and the next after that, we did it all over again. Of course, there wasn't quite so much to eat after the first day, but the Indians didn't care. They were used to having a big feast, and then not bothering much about food for several days. But even at that it kept us busy cooking. We didn't mind because we had plenty, and if it meant peace and goodwill between ourselves and the Indians, we women were only too glad to do our part to help. But when it was all over and the Indians finally left, we had to do a lot of cleaning up. Soon after that the cold shut down on us and our second winter in Plymouth began. So that," said Grandma, "is the story of our First Thanksgiving.

"It was a good Thanksgiving, and ever since your Grandpa and I were married two years later we have had Thanksgiving in our home, and we've always made the Indians welcome too.

We haven't always had as much as we have now, but we've shared what we had gladly. I hope the time will come in this good land when everyone will be truly thankful in this way that has brought us so much satisfaction. Remember this, children, all your lives long: Whatever you have, be it much or little, share your comfort and plenty, and let no one go cold or hungry."

Grandma was tired now, and her voice was low. A log fell and flames blazed up, lighting the intent faces of her listeners. No one spoke for a minute, and then Uncle William broke the silence in his great booming voice:

"Mother," he said, "I haven't been home at harvest time for near twenty years, but when I am off in foreign lands, or wherever I be come harvest time, I think of your Thanksgiving at home. And our little Hannah here, I warrant her mother remembers, too, and tells her children. Is that so, little one?"

"Yes, Uncle William, she does every year, but she says that's not the same as being here, and hearing Grandma tell us her story."

"She's right, too, and now come and eat some

of these nice roasted chestnuts. Ouch! these ashes are hot! Mind you don't burn your fingers! Come on, children, all who are going home in the cold, eat a nice hot apple before you go. Jonathan, I've got a parcel of foreign truck for you, figs and raisins and such if you can pack it home."

"That's right kind of you, William. 'Twill be a rare treat for the children, and Hattie can use some in her cooking. There's nothing like raisins to make a tasty pudding more tasty. And now I must get the nags. The sun is low, and we must be home by the time the dark creeps under the table. Goodbye, Mother, we've had a good Thanksgiving. We thank you, and we'll bide by what you told us."

Her goodbyes said, Hannah trotted along by Uncle Jonathan's side when he went to the barn to get the horses, for she must get her kitten. She chose the gray one at last, and Aunt Joy found a basket for the kitten to travel in.

"What will you name her, Hannah?" asked Content, when safe in Uncle Jonathan's kitchen the kitten was daintily lapping a saucer of milk.

"I've named her Thankful," said Hannah, "because she's a Thanksgiving cat, and this Thanksgiving day is the nicest day I've ever spent."

A Note on the Type

IN WHICH THIS BOOK IS SET

This book was set on the Linotype in Janson, a recutting made direct from the type cast from matrices (now in possession of the Stempel foundry, Frankfurt am Main) made by Anton Janson some time between 1660 and 1687.

Of Janson's origin nothing is known. He may have been a relative of Justus Janson, a printer of Danish birth who practised in Leipzig from 1614 to 1635. Some time between 1657 and 1668 Anton Janson, a punch-cutter and type-founder, bought from the Leipzig printer Johann Erich Hahn the type-foundry which had formerly been a part of the printing house of M. Friedrich Lankisch. Janson's types were first shown in a specimen sheet issued at Leipzig about 1675. Janson's successor, and perhaps his son-in-law, Johann Karl Edling, issued a specimen sheet of Janson types in 1689. His heirs sold the Janson matrices in Holland to Wolffgang Dietrich Erhardt, of Leipzig.

COMPOSED, PRINTED, AND BOUND BY
H. Wolff, NEW YORK, N. Y.